*Piano · Vocal · Guitar*

# JOHNNY CASH
## *My Mother's Hymn Book*

ISBN 978-0-634-08383-9

**HAL•LEONARD®**
**CORPORATION**
7777 W. BLUEMOUND RD. P.O. BOX 13819 MILWAUKEE, WI 53213

Visit Hal Leonard Online at

# contents

# WHERE WE'LL NEVER GROW OLD

Words and Music by
JAMES C. MOORE

Nev - er grow __ old, where we'll nev - er grow __ old, _____ in a

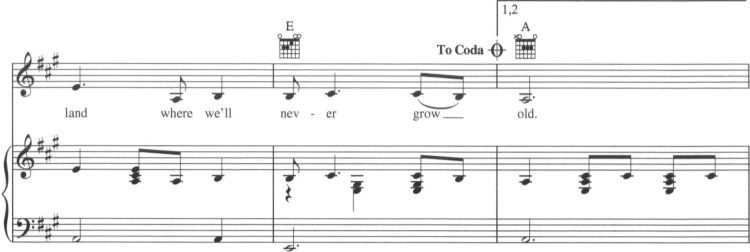

land where we'll nev - er grow __ old.

In that old.
When our

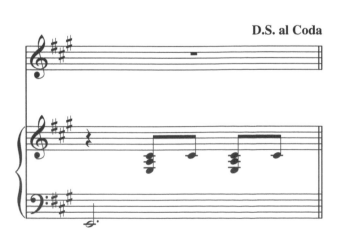

**D.S. al Coda**

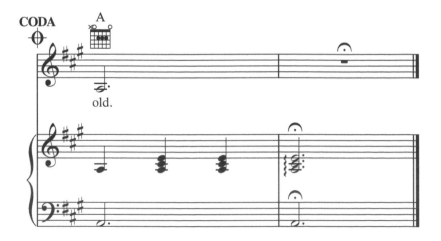

old.

# I SHALL NOT BE MOVED

Words and Music by
V.O. FOSSETT

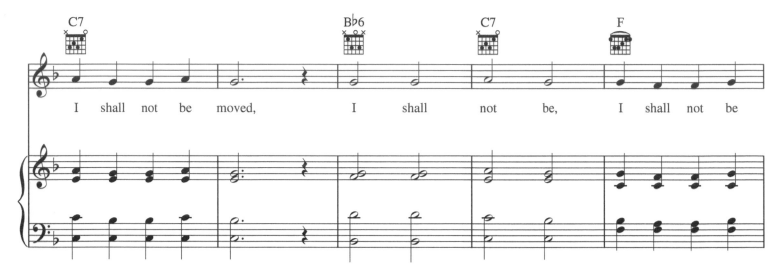

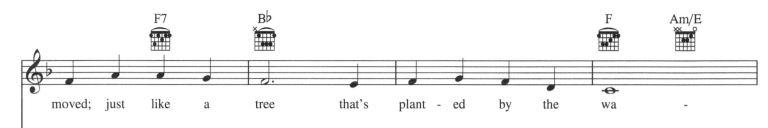

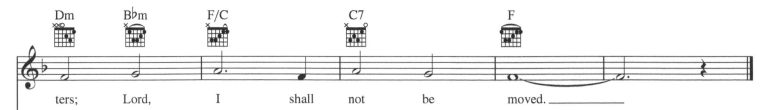

# I AM A PILGRIM

Words and Music by
MERLE TRAVIS

10

I am ___ de - ter - mined ___ to go ___ and
If I ___ can just touch ___ the hem ___ of His

**G7**

see them, ___ good Lord, ___ o - ver on ___
gar - ment, ___ good Lord, ___ then I know ___

**D**

**A**

**D**

1

that oth - er shore. ___
He'll take ___ me home. ___

I am a

2

**D.S. al Coda**

I am a

**CODA**

**A**

**D**

not made ___ by hand. ___

# DO LORD

Words and Music by
V.O. FOSSETT

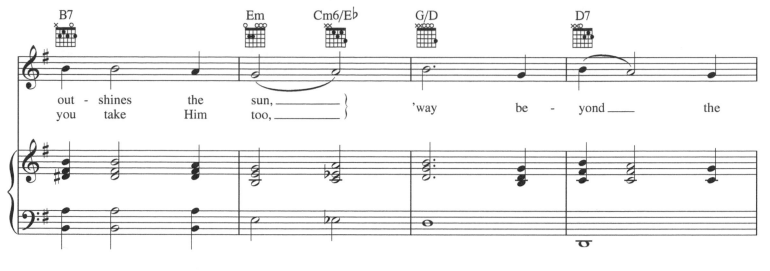

out - shines the sun, _____ } 'way be - yond _____ the
you take the Him too, _____ }

blue. Do Lord, oh, do Lord, oh,

do re - mem - ber me. Do Lord, oh,

do Lord, oh, do re - mem - ber me.

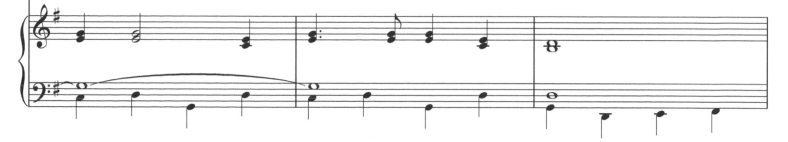

# WHEN THE ROLL IS CALLED UP YONDER

Traditional
Arranged by JOHN R. CASH

there! }
there! }
When the roll _____ is called up yon - der, When the

roll _____ is called up yon - der, When the roll _____ is called up

yon - der, When the roll is called up yon - der, I'll be there! On that

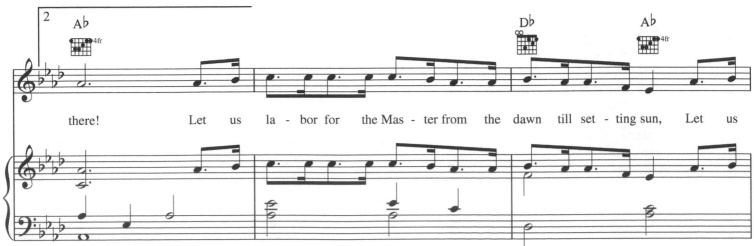

there! Let us la - bor for the Mas - ter from the dawn till set - ting sun, Let us

# IF WE NEVER MEET AGAIN

Words and Music by
ALBERT E. BRUMLEY

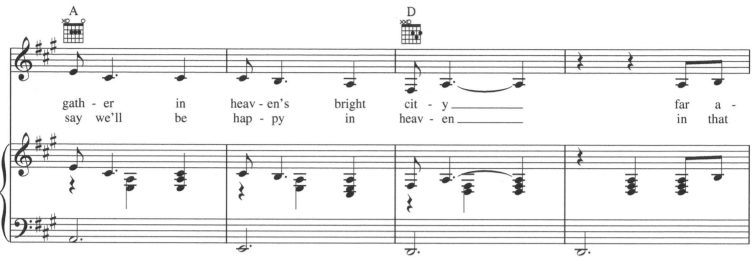

gath - er in heav - en's bright cit - y _____ far a -
say we'll be hap - py in heav - en _____ in that

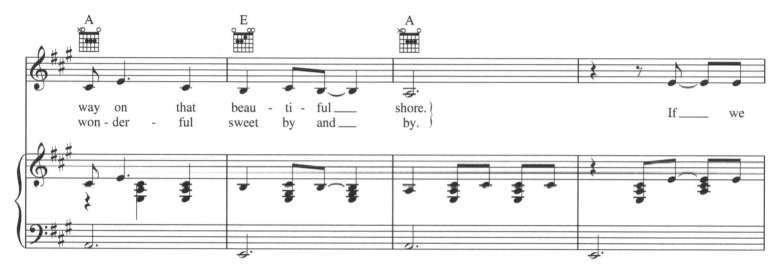

way on that beau - ti - ful ___ shore.
won - der - ful sweet by and ___ by.
If ___ we

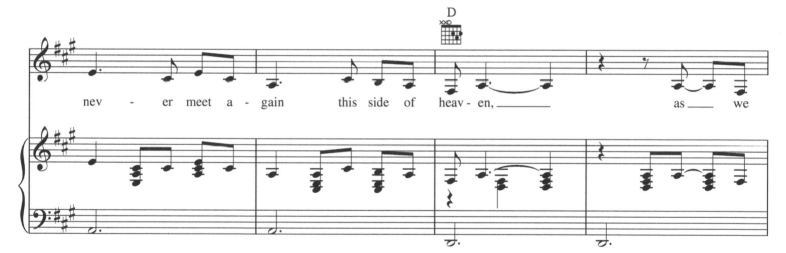

nev - er meet a - gain this side of heav - en, _____ as ___ we

strug - gle through this world and its ___ strife, there's ___ an -

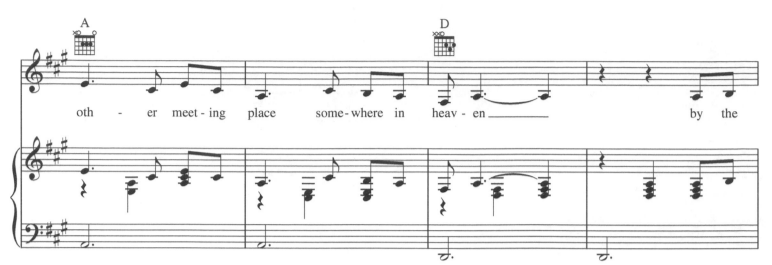

oth - er meet - ing place some - where in heav - en _____ by the

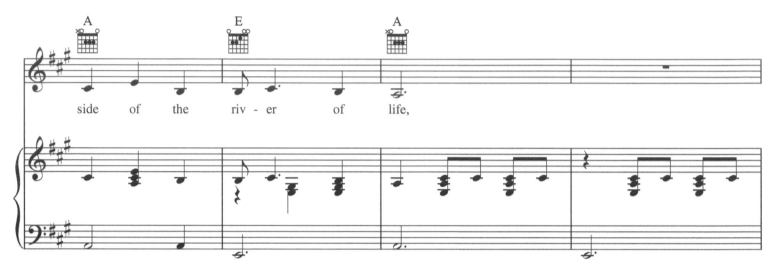

side of the riv - er of life,

where the ros - es bloom _____ for - ev - er _____ and ___ where

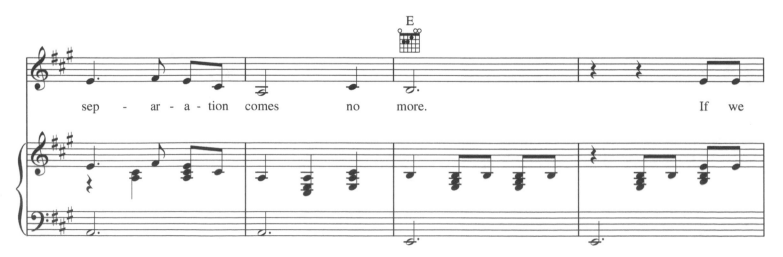

sep - ar - a - tion comes no more. If we

# I'LL FLY AWAY

Words and Music by
ALBERT E. BRUMLEY

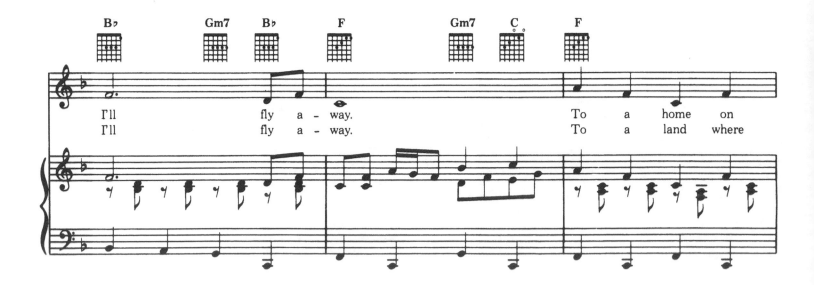

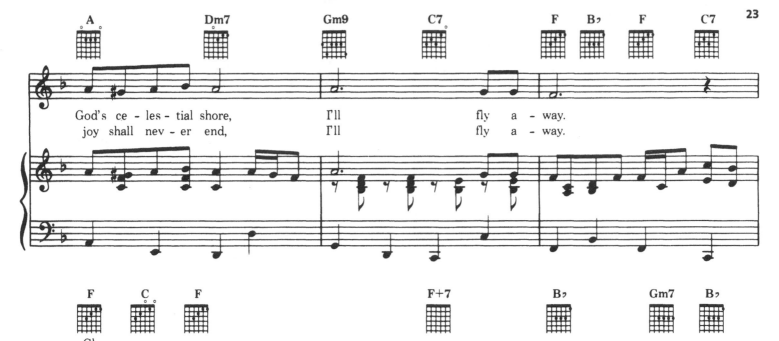

God's ce - les - tial shore,      I'll      fly  a - way.
joy shall nev - er end,      I'll      fly  a - way.

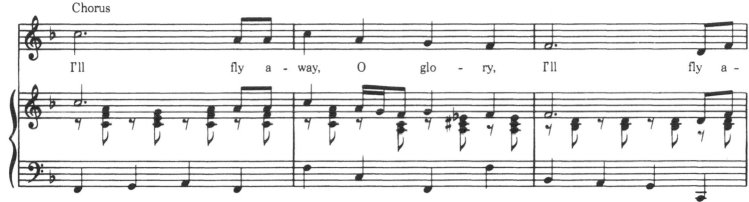

Chorus

I'll      fly a - way,  O  glo - ry,  I'll      fly a -

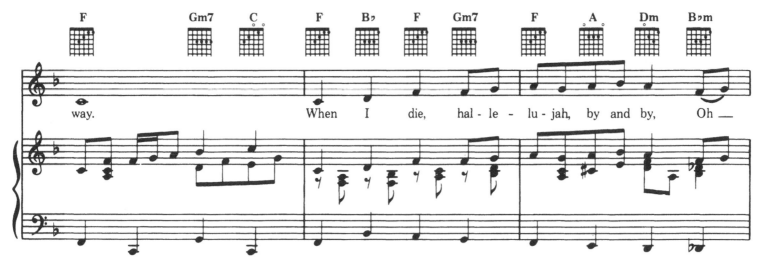

way.      When I die, hal - le - lu - jah, by and by,  Oh __

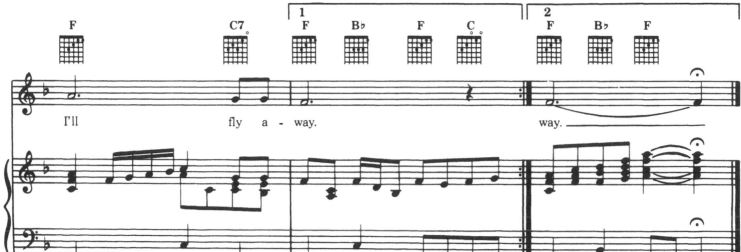

1.
I'll      fly a - way.

2.
way. _____

# WHERE THE SOUL
# OF MAN NEVER DIES

Traditional
Arranged by JOHN R. CASH

dark - est \_\_\_\_ night will turn to \_\_\_\_ day where the
I will \_\_\_\_ spend e - ter - ni - ty where the
there will \_\_\_\_ be no part - ing \_\_\_\_ hand, and the

soul of man nev - er dies.
soul of man nev - er dies.       Dear
soul of man nev - er dies.

friends, there'll \_ be no sad fare - well, there'll

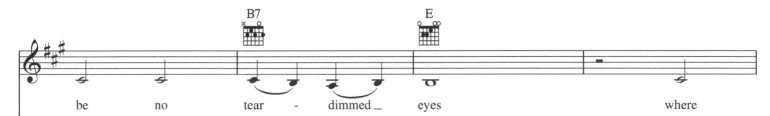

be no tear - dimmed \_ eyes       where

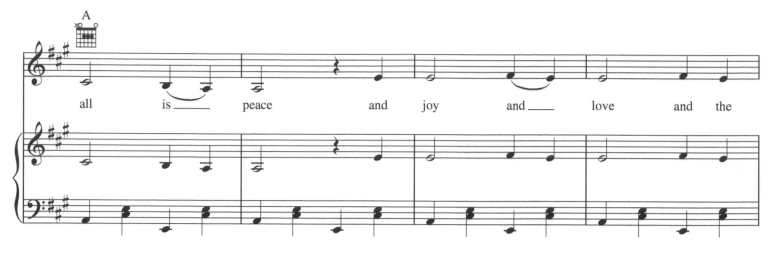

all is ____ peace and joy and ____ love and the

soul of man nev - er dies.

A soul of
I'm

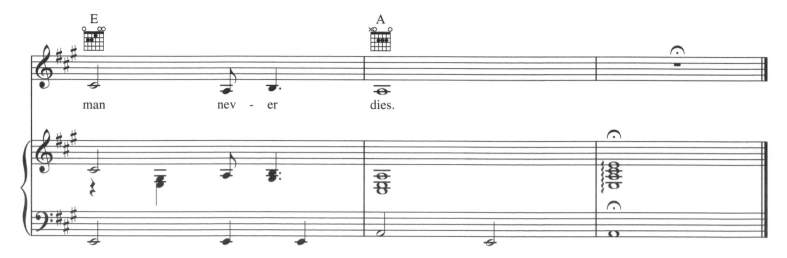

man nev - er dies.

# LET THE LOWER LIGHTS BE BURNING

Traditional
Arrangement by JOHNNY CASH

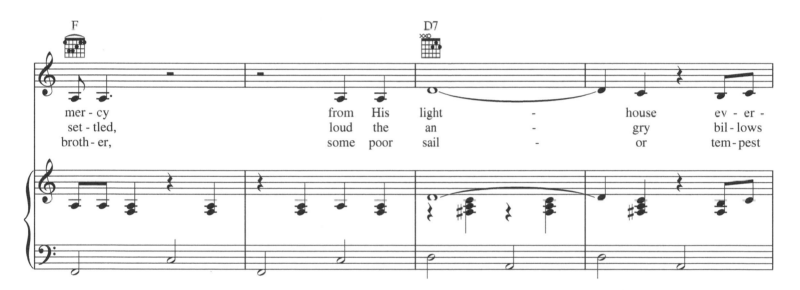

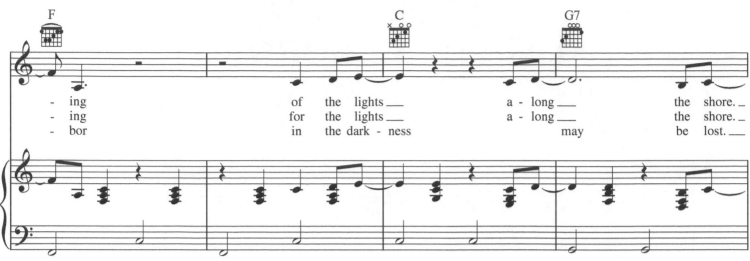

-ing                     of the lights ___            a - long ___           the shore. __
-ing                     for the lights ___            a - long ___           the shore. __
-bor                     in the dark - ness             may          be lost. ___

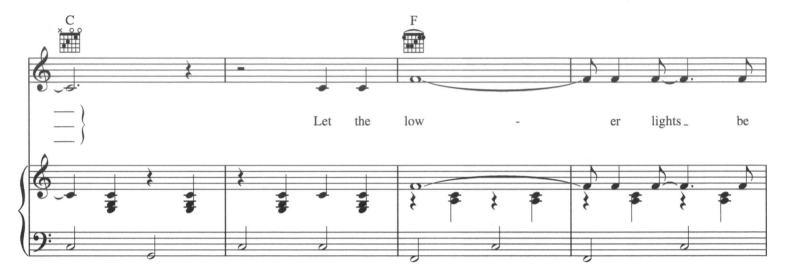

Let the low - er lights __ be

burn - ing,                     send the gleam _____

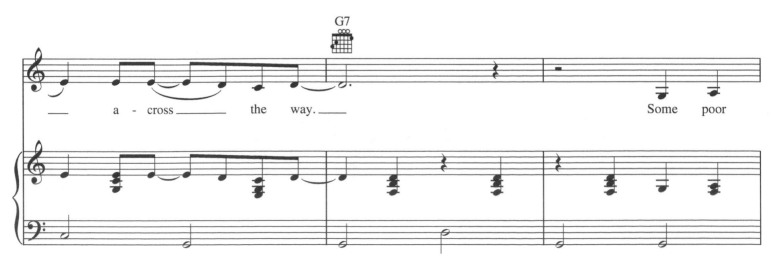

___ a - cross _____ the way. ___                   Some poor

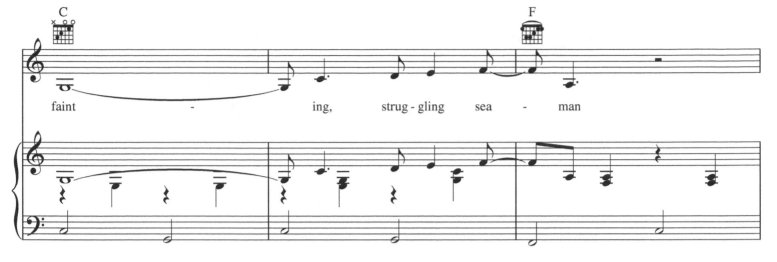

faint - ing, strug - gling sea - man

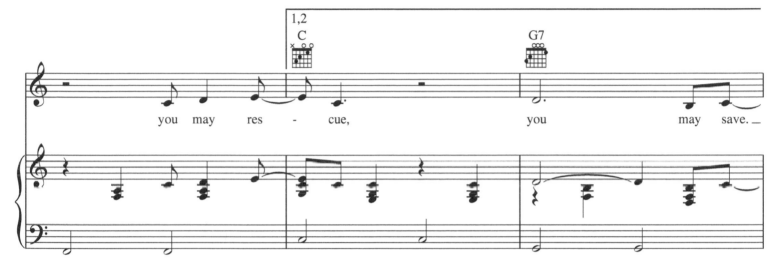

1,2

you may res - cue, you may save. __

3

Dark the night __ - cue, __
Trim your fee -

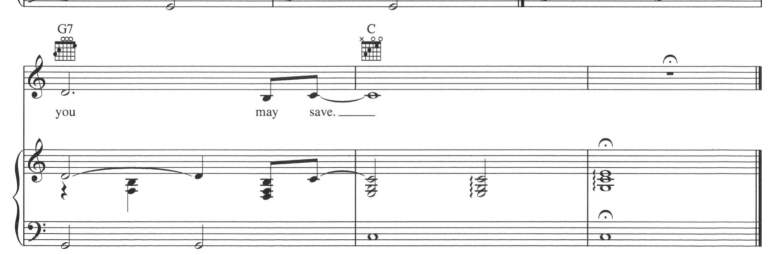

you may save. __

# WHEN HE REACHED DOWN HIS HAND FOR ME

Words and Music by J.F.B. WRIGHT,
MARION EASTERLING and THOMAS

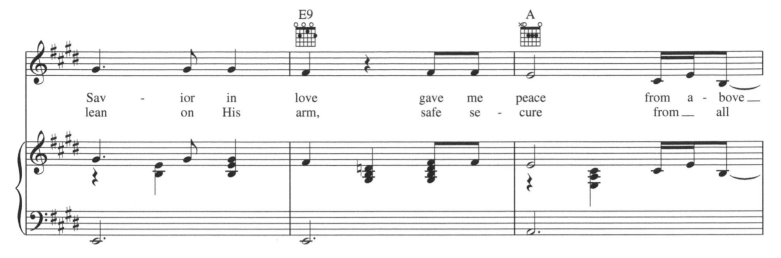

me,                    I was lost _____ and un-done ____        with-out

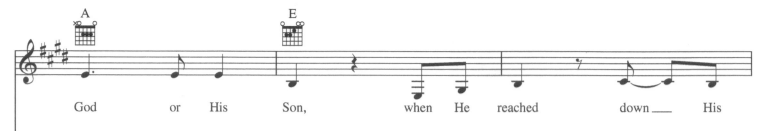

God        or  His    Son,        when He reached      down ____    His

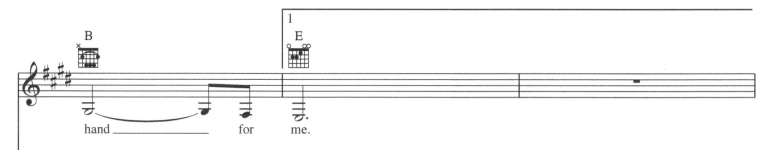

hand _____ for   me.

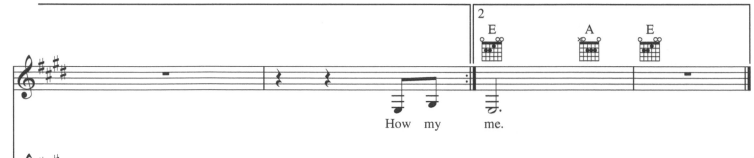

How  my          me.

# IN THE SWEET BY AND BY

Traditional
Arranged by JOHN R. CASH

Cheerfully

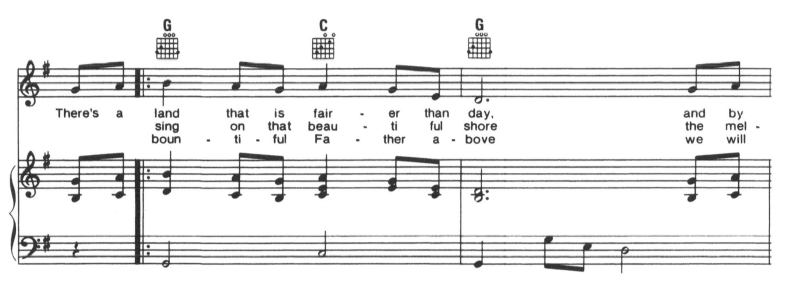

There's a land that is fair - er than day, and by
sing on that beau - ti - ful shore the mel -
boun - ti - ful Fa - ther a - bove we will

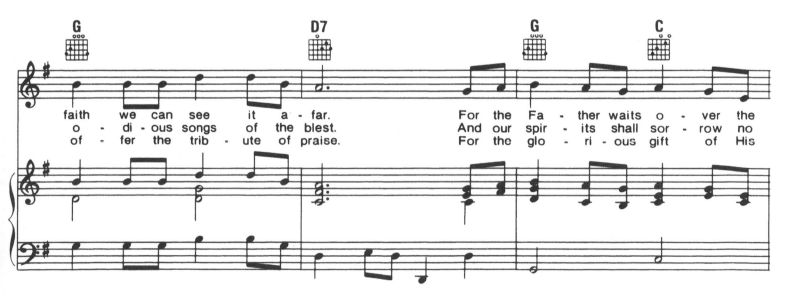

faith we can see it a - far. For the Fa - ther waits o - ver the
o - di - ous songs of the blest. And our spir - its shall sor - row no
of - fer the trib - ute of praise. For the glo - ri - ous gift of His

# I'M BOUND FOR THE PROMISED LAND

Traditional
Arranged by John R. Cash

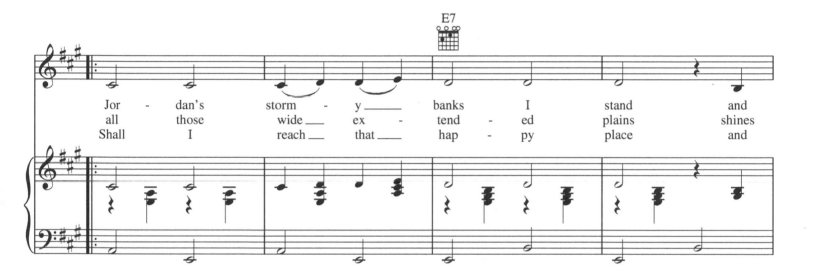

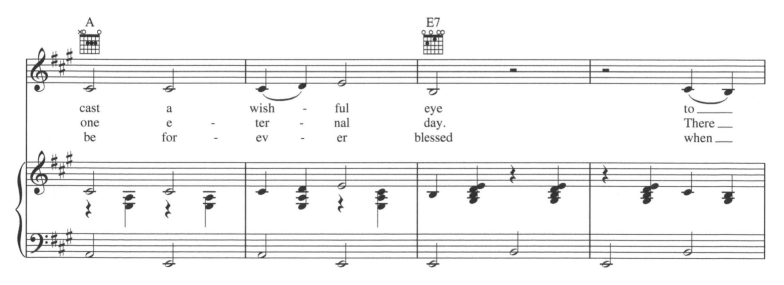

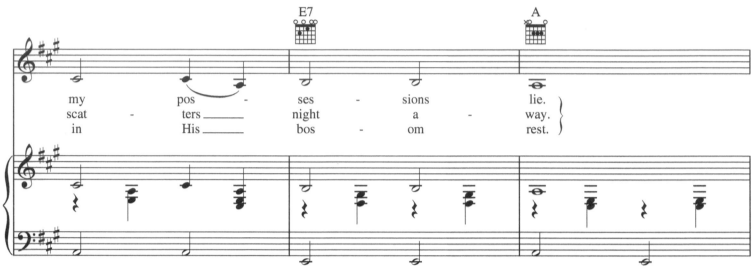

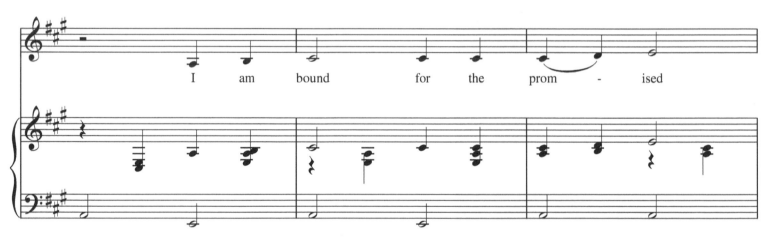

# IN THE GARDEN

Words and Music by
C. AUSTIN MILES

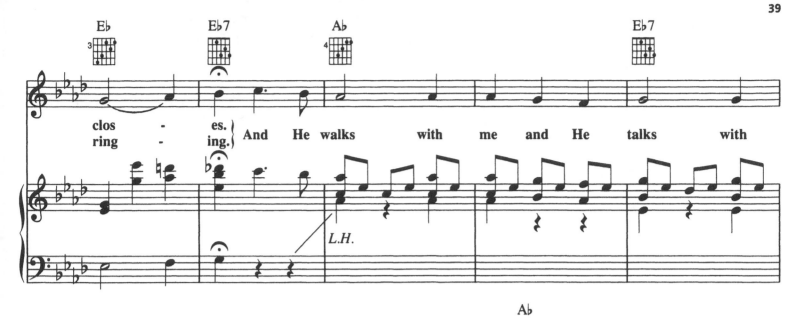

clos - es.
ring - ing. } And He walks with me and He talks with

me, and He tells me I am His own;_____ and the

joy we share as we tar - ry there, none oth - er has

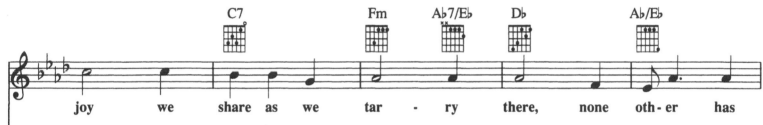

ev - er _____ known. _____ He known. _____

# SOFTLY AND TENDERLY

Traditional
Arranged by JOHN R. CASH

Moderately Slow

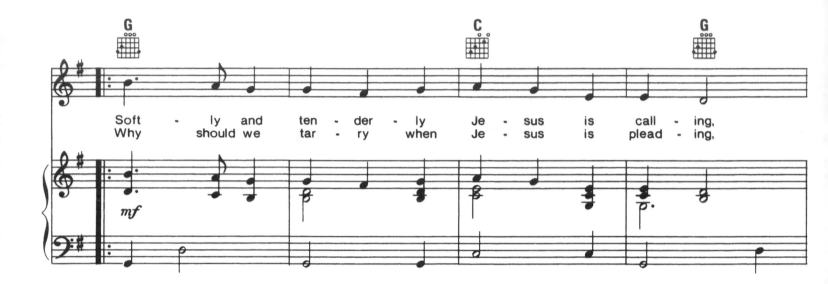

Soft - ly and ten - der - ly Je - sus is call - ing,
Why should we tar - ry when Je - sus is plead - ing,

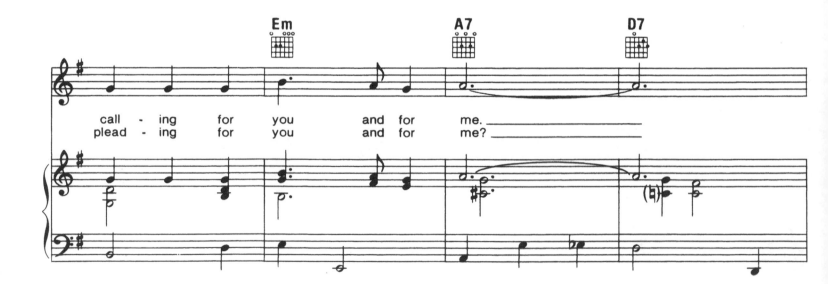

call - ing for you and for me. _____
plead - ing for you and for me? _____

# JUST AS I AM

Traditional
Arranged by JOHN R. CASH

Slowly, with movement

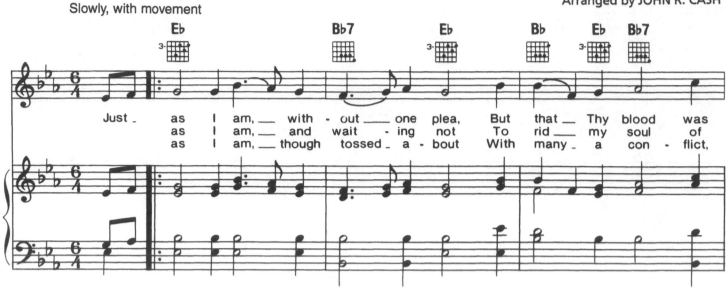

Just _ as I am, __ with - out __ one plea, But that __ Thy blood was
as I am, __ and wait - ing not To rid __ my soul was
as I am, __ though tossed _ a - bout With many _ a con - flict,

shed for me, And _ that Thou bidd'st __ me come to Thee, __ O
one dark blot, To __ Thee whose blood __ can cleanse each spot, __ O
many a doubt, Fight - ings and fears __ with - in, with - out __ O

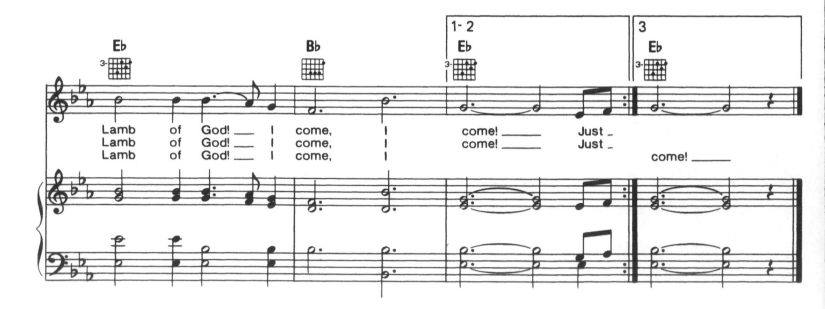

Lamb of God! __ I come, I come! _____ Just _
Lamb of God! __ I come, I come! _____ Just _
Lamb of God! __ I come, I come!